LAMELO E

CW00508241

HOW LAMELO BALL BECAME THE NBA'S

MOST EXCITING PLAYER

By

JACKSON CARTER

TABLE OF CONTENTS

LEGAL NOTES

LaMelo Ball is meant for entertainment and educational use only. All attempts have been made to present factual information in an unbiased context.

LaMelo Ball

The youngest of the world-famous players, LaMelo plays point guard and stands 6'7" (2.01 m.). That doesn't include his tall hair, by the way. "Ever since I was little, when I'd do little projects and stuff, that was one of my goals--to go to the NBA and be the No. 1 pick," LaMelo stated in a Combine interview just before the 2020 player draft.

In a nutshell, LaMelo entered the post-pandemic NBA Draft as one of the most publicized, highly anticipated picks ever. All this and the Ball kid is still only 19.

To say his life's been a whirlwind is an understatement. He is the son of the irrepressible LaVar Ball, a former pro football player, and mother, Tina (who also played college hoops). His oldest brother, Lonzo, plays with the NBA Pelicans. Simultaneously, the next oldest, LiAngelo, has also played pro in Lithuania and the NBA "G (Development) League".

LaMelo's still a teen, but his father has already yanked him out of the line to play at UCLA, moved him to Lithuania and then Australia to play, created a league called the JBA for him to star in, and designed a signature shoe for him, the "Melo Ball 1" (as part of the family's "Big Baller Brand"). Coincidentally, LaMelo is a celeb. Melo has some 5.6 million followers on Instagram, more than established pros like Luka Doncic, Joel Embiid, and Jayson Tatum. He plays a part in the Facebook Watch reality show, "Ball In The Family". He admits, "It's always been like this."

LaMELO'S EARLY LIFE

His father stuck a basketball in Melo's hands when he could barely walk. LaVar was his sons' first coach and he worked them out practically from birth. Outside their previous, slightly smaller home (the current one is a monster, with a living room only that cost $100K) in Chino Hills, the kids came back after school and jumped into what looked like a basketball camp. The three Ball brothers, neighborhood pals, and the children of LaVar's friends from around Los Angeles all made the scene. They ran lots of hills, sweated through shooting drills, and played 3-on-3 until after dark.

"He was tough on all three of us," LaMelo admitted. Then he thought again and said, "I wouldn't even say tough, though. But if you were just a random person seeing him coach us, you'd be like, 'What the *hell*?'"

At the age of six, Melo jumped from the top of a high wall into the family's backyard pool. "Y'all, this is funnnnnnnnnnnn!" he screamed at his brothers. But a moment later, he slipped from the wall and fell hard. He could barely walk, so his middle brother, Gelo, gave him piggyback rides for the remainder of the week. LaMelo remembers LaVar shouting at Gelo, "Why the f--k are you giving this dude a piggy ride? Put his ass down!" Yet, when LaMelo tried to walk, his ankle pulsated in pain. LaVar said it didn't matter; he had to walk through the pain. Tough love indeed.

Growing up, LaMelo played with his two older brothers on Amateur Athletic Union (AAU) teams coached by LaVar. The teams boasted the distinct name "Big Ballers VXT," a hint at the family's future shoe company. Like many domineering dads, LaVar gladly took the coaching reins. Unlike many, the elder Ball had a substantial athletic pedigree, playing college hoops for Washington State and then Cal State Los Angeles. He also had a stint in pro football as a tight end with none other than the London Monarchs, racking up 28 kickoff return yards and zero receptions. Finally, he was a member of the NY Jets and Carolina Panthers practice squads in 1995.

It also helps to have a dad who can carry his weight, even though at times he may get a little loud. LaMelo recalls an afternoon in a gym in one of LA's rough neighborhoods when he was four. He was shooting off to the side with LaVar while Lonzo and Gelo played pickup with grown men. Someone committed a hard foul and a verbal dispute started. "All right! All right! I'mma be back!" one man shouted threateningly. Indeed, he came back soon enough, squeezing in through the back door, wearing a black hoodie and carrying a loaded gun. "Shot the whole gym up," LaMelo says. "Pop pop pop pop." Melo marvels at how, in a split second, his feet dangled in the air, his tiny figure protected by his father's body. LaVar had somehow grabbed him, Lonzo, and Gelo in his arms, cradling all three boys while running hard out of the gym to safety.

LaVar was always keen for LaMelo to play against bigger and older opponents, starting with his brothers and extending to his time in frigid Lithuania with Prienai and the Illawarra Hawks of the far-flung Australian NBL while still a teen. As a five-year-old, he also played flag football with his brothers but always keyed in on basketball. Maybe Melo would disagree entirely, but his two older brothers (separated by 13 months) were physically stronger. Four years younger than his eldest sibling, Lonzo, the brothers' baby came home from the hospital in 2001. LaMelo LaFrance Ball has had to fight to keep pace ever since.

From the start, LaVar seemed harder on Melo than anyone else. Straight away, the boy received his room, right next to his parents. Mother Tina took him under her wing, but Melo had to keep the room clean, and he had to keep up with his high-flying brothers continually. He had to speak up, and so he did, even becoming a little loud like his dad. Lonzo's jump shot has been criticized as unorthodox and easily blocked. But Melo Dips (as his dad originally called him) can be called even uglier from a purist's standpoint: a unique two-handed push shot that, in the end, has given him the range to shoot from midcourt (as you'll get to know later) and brought quick comparisons to the venerable three-point king, Steph Curry.

As early as four years old, LaVar pushed Melo to shoot with a regulation ball on a 10-foot hoop. The youngster recorded his first half-court shot at age six. By seven, he'd hit half-courters regularly. The shooting form stuck, and he started shooting with two hands from every spot on the floor. He learned he could better control the ball with two hands and take advantage of a quicker release. What was first torn down as defective by youth coaches and scouts suddenly became a decided edge, with Melo hitting shots from ridiculous range without working up a sweat—and without hitting the weights. Even now, at 19, his skinny limbs and thin chest don't allow him to bench press much.

But he's finally filling out and apparently will soon be lighting it up in the NBA. Not too long ago, he was only five, and kids were already waiting in line for his autograph while he played with his older brothers. It seems his gifted ball-handling skills even at that age were already news at the middle school where mother Tina worked. When he was ten, he was supposed to outplay others five or six years his senior. He remembered another time when he was 14, playing for Chino Hills High, and an unknown man came out of nowhere offering to pay for his order at Yogurtland. The man was happy to pay—he knew how highly Melo was ranked.

LaMelo's Famous Family

Their father, LaVar, is no stranger to the spotlight. First, he claimed in 2015 that Lonzo was "Magic (Johnson) with a jump shot". Then in 2017, he publicly surmised he could make mincemeat of Michael Jordan playing one on one. That raised a few chuckles as pundits pointed out his less-than-gaudy stats as a college hoopster at Washington State: 2.2 points, 2.3 rebounds, and one assist per game. He then stated that Lonzo was better than Steph Curry, had a go at the Lakers for their rough treatment of his oldest son, exchanged words with Donald Trump after LiAngelo was nabbed shoplifting in China, all of the above while championing his Big Baller Brand and starting the JBA for Gelo and Melo to play in (naturally after they'd both lost their amateur status—Melo as a 16-year-old when he first donned his signature sneaker made by his dad's big brand).

Mother Tina was recently the athletic director at Vernon Middle School in Montclair, California. She married LaVar, her college sweetheart, who quipped, "I transferred from Washington State (to Cal State, L.A.) and saw her in the hall. Wow. She knocked me off my feet. I stopped her in the hall and said, "I don't know what we're going to do together, but we're gonna do something." She was like, "Is this guy cocky or what?" "Tina put up some impressive stats herself as a high school senior, snagging 18.2 rebounds per game and finished fourth in career rebounds at Cal State with 627.

Only six months after the Balls went global with their "Ball in The Family" reality show, and during Lonzo's freshman year at UCLA, Tina suffered a stroke. She has dealt with aphasia (the loss of the ability to understand or express speech caused by brain damage) ever since. Yet, two years later, Tina has kept battling and recovered some of her physical control—all shown in detail on the show. LaMelo remains upbeat: "My mom, we'll be in the gym for 10 hours, and she'll be there. I think that's what really got it. Everyone has fun when we play basketball. But watching us play is pretty much a date for her."

Lonzo will always be the first. He broke the single-season assist record in his first and only year at UCLA, leading the nation in assists the same year. He went second overall in the 2017 NBA Draft, although injuries hampered his two short years with the Lakers. Lonzo was then traded to the Pelicans in Lebron's LA shake-up that brought the towering Anthony Davis to the City of Angels—and the Lakers' first championship in 10 years, tying the Celtics as the NBA's all-time elite with 17 titles. Before the big time, Lonzo led Chino Hills High to a 35–0 record and the state title in his senior year, with the Huskies rated the consensus No. 1 team in the country. His younger brothers, junior LiAngelo and freshman LaMelo, as well as his cousin, Andre, were all on board for the team's wild ride.

Middle brother, LiAngelo Robert Ball, ended up a bit shorter than the other two at 6'5" (1.96 m.). He was a

UCLA signee, but grabbed a suspension prior to the 2017-18 season for his Chinese shoplifting escapade. Gelo gave up on college hoops as a result and signed with Lithuanian club Prienai alongside Melo. He later bolted for the Junior Basketball Association (JBA) started by his dad and moved on to the "G League" with the Oklahoma Blue at the end of 2019-20. Obviously, all the brothers can hoop it and LaVar keeps dreaming of the Ball name in big bright lights: "If everything lines up right and the Knicks get the first pick and get LaMelo and LiAngelo with him and somehow get Lonzo in the long run. Shoot—the Triple B's. The Ball Brothers on Broadway."

MELO HIGH SCHOOL DAYS

Entering Chino Hills High (CA) as a 5-foot-10 freshman starter, Melo was still a baby-faced guard. But his flash the previous summer had already gained him substantial social media attention. Including Melo, everybody knew the team was led by Lonzo (who would go on to become the "Mr. Basketball USA" choice as the national player of the year for 2015-16). Melo picked his offensive spots and didn't attempt too much on a team showcasing two 14-year-olds (the other was current USC recruit and Chino Hills senior Onyeka Okongwu). They wrapped up the season at 35-0, ranked No. 1 in the nation, and finally led the land in fire code violations due to their jammed gym. In his debut as a frosh, LaMelo notched 27 points. His reaction? "It was a fast-paced game," he said. Big bro Lonzo countered, "He should have had 30."

In the following campaign (2016-17), Melo was one of four returning starters from the mythical national championship team of Chino Hills. On the one hand, he was touted as a Top 20 prospect nationally in the 2019 class of soaring sophomores. On the other, this was the season in which he started showing signs that he might have legit NBA potential. He already stood at 6-foot-1 (pushing 6'2"), and with Lonzo off to university, he had the ball in his hands most of the time. Melo was increasingly explosive around the hoop, showed an increased ability to score, and kept up a good measure of razzle-dazzle that seemed to help more often than hurt his team.

Chino Hills ran off 60 straight wins to challenge the greatest California high school streak of all time (Compton High had snatched 66 straight from 1967 to '69) before tumbling to Oak Hill Academy (Wilson, VA) in the 2017 Nike Extravaganza. Even in defeat, some said that Melo may have had his best outing as a high-schooler with 35 points and constantly attacking the paint against a talented team of seniors, most headed for the NCAA's D1. On the day, he received multiple nods from McDonald's All-American voters as a 2019 Top 15 recruit.

Then the next game happened. Melo went off for 92 points (including 41 in the fourth only) against Los Osos. According to Southern Cal News Group's Tommy Kiss, Ball hit a sizzling 30 of 39 two-pointers, although he was slightly less impressive on threes (7 of 22). He connected on 11 of 14 from the charity stripe and added seven assists and five rebounds to top it off. First came the accolades: "Between his personality, a penchant for the absurd on the floor, and his hair, LaMelo Ball is going to be an incredibly fun player to track," gushed Sam Vecenie of the Sporting News.

Soon though, Melo began to receive the kind of public scorn reserved for those much older than 15. Los Osos coach, Dave Smith, called Ball's performance "a joke" afterward, according to the LA Times. "Chino Hills players had intentionally fouled Los Osos players to stop the clock when Los Osos was on offense, thereby giving Ball more time to pad his point total,"

Smith said in the Times interview. Closer video analysis showed the young Ball constantly committing the major basketball no-no of "cherry-picking," clearly not bothering to get back on D so that he could grab a long pass off a rebound from a teammate for an easy two.

"That's wrong," Smith said to the Times. "It goes against everything CIF (California Interscholastic Federation) stands for. The Ball boys are very talented and great players, but it's embarrassing to high school athletics. I've been coaching for 35 years and we've turned high school athletics into individualism. It's amazing to watch a kid score that many points. But it's tough to say that's what CIF athletics is about." Before Melo's polemical production, the Ball name had already been questioned earlier in the season when LiAngelo, a senior at Chino Hills, had torched Rancho Christian for 72 of his team's 128 points.

Maybe it's necessary to backpedal a bit. On December 26, 2016, during Chino Hills 47th straight win against Foothill, Melo calmly caught an inbounds pass just short of the halfway line. He dribbled while pointing down at the line twice and then launched an improbable moonshot from beyond half-court. The ball swished through and the gym roared. By the way, the youngest Ball had 65 points in that Rancho Mirage Holiday International game. A day later, the clip of the 15-year-old's sky shot went viral, and Melo has recorded almost 2 million views on YouTube to date.

Back to the 92-point effort: critics besides Coach Smith stated that Melo's play seemed planned along the lines of what he previously showed while sporting the "Big Ballers VXT" uniform. When he was in seventh grade, Melo played with his brothers on an AAU team formed by his parents that hooped it on the So Cali Circuit. VXT comes from the so-called "Virtual Xtreme Technique" pioneered by basketball guru, Provat Gupta, son of former "Good Times" star, Ja'net Dubois who played the character, Willona Woods. Gupta turns out to be a street hoops legend from the Big Apple who made his way to LA. The VXT skillset "allows players to learn to score from all areas of the court". And from the VXT hype itself: The VXT workout "will provide young athletes the tools needed to score like 9th-grade LaMelo Ball did for Chino Hills".

During LaMelo's young life, the strong hand of his father has always existed. Not only did his dad form an AAU team for him and his brothers, and more recently set up an entire league for them as well (the JBA), but he's also had a number of run-ins with his boys' coaches. Shortly after Melo's 92-point outburst, LaVar's relationship with rookie Chino Hills head coach, Stephan Gilling became increasingly strained. Finally, in Chino's CIF Southern Section semifinal defeat versus Mater Dei of Santa Ana (CA), with many of Melo's shot attempts labeled "ridiculous," the tenuous connection snapped.

In November 2018, LaMelo Ball reappeared far from the Golden State for his senior year at the SPIRE Academy in Geneva, Ohio. His numbers didn't disappoint: 20.4 points a game on 55.3% shooting from the field, together with 9 rebounds and 9.1 assists, according to Prep Circuit. Those stats looked remarkably similar to Lonzo's last prep year at Chino Hills (23.9 ppg, 11.3 rebounds, and 11.5 assists per game). Despite the swirling controversy in his high school career, Melo demonstrated he could still perform at a high level for a talented team, while media attention and pressure continued to mount.

Melo had effectively missed his junior year and part of his senior year of high school to play pro. But since SPIRE competed outside the Ohio High School Athletic Association's jurisdiction, Melo was allowed to jump in. Numerous well-known high school teams opted out of their games against SPIRE and head coach, Jermaine Jackson, because they feared their state federation eligibility could be jeopardized by Ball's stints as a pro. SPIRE was also pulled from the Hoophall Classic Tournament as event organizers didn't cough up the $10,000 requested by a Ball family associate for Melo to strut his stuff.

When Melo had his coming-out party for SPIRE on November 10, 2018, he chipped in 20 points, 13 assists, and 5 rebounds as his team handily toppled The Hill School (PA), 96-84. On March 7, 2019, the young Ball ripped off 29 in the first half and finished with 41 as the SPIRE squad romped past Hillcrest Prep North (AZ), 102-67, at the Grind Session World Championship. Although SPIRE would eventually fall in the Final to Bella Vista Prep (AZ), 96-94, in a wild finish, with Prep's players leaving the bench to celebrate before the game officially finished. Even though they were not assessed technical fouls en masse because of their action, Melo was named tournament MVP. He started slowly in the Final, only hitting his first shot two minutes before the half. Ball ended up with 25 on 5-of-15 shooting from the field. Ultimately, he was ruled out of the 2019 McDonald's All-American Game due to his experience as a pro.

Prep school SPIRE seemed a good fit at the time for Melo. The "professional preparatory experience" for basketball, swimming, and track and field (as well as camp programs for soccer, eSports, and even drones) allows the academy to work with "ambassadors" such as LaMelo, Ryan Lochte, Elizabeth Beisel, and Tianna Bartoletta "to emphasize the development of peak performance in athletics, academics, character, and life". Remarkably, LaMelo stayed calm amidst all the high school moves and spoke candidly about what changed and what remained the same—namely his confidence during his prep days: "I got taller, so I can rebound now. Better on defense, but still working on defense. I'm blessed on defense but you know, you do the offense and you are tired. For the defense, you are going to lack a little. That's where that comes from. But if I were to score zero points, I promise you, nobody's scoring on me."

Prienai, Lithuania

Prienai, Lithuania, is a world away from Chino Hills, California. But LaVar Ball always claimed that ball is life or more appropriately, business. The Ball patriarch plucked his two younger sons, LiAngelo and LaMelo, from sunny Southern Cal to play pro in that cold, faraway Baltic state. Just before the long-distance move, LaVar had hinted that he considered LiAngelo his least talented son in terms of hoops, while LaMelo was widely regarded as a top high school prospect (in the US, if not the world). They arrived on January 3, 2018 to tremendous fanfare. Other American players who had gone before compared the rural town to life on a farm: no restaurants or malls to speak of, but no traffic problems either. The players normally stayed at the Royal SPA Residence in Birstonas, a mere 10 minutes from the arena.

"You can count on one hand the number of street lights in that city," said veteran American pro player, Billy Baron, who spent his rookie year at Rytas Vilnius in Europe toiling for the man who was the Ball brothers' latest coach, Virginijus Seskus. "There is nothing to do in that place. It's the ultimate life of going to practice and back to the hotel." On the other hand, imagine the local Lithuanians when the Ball circus pulled into town. "The first month was completely crazy. Everything was new. Everything was kind of shocking. Everything was kind of exciting. We were following what the Ball brothers and what LaVar was saying. What are they going to say about

Lithuania--every step, every move, every word, every new experience in Lithuania was something fun," exclaimed Donatas Urbonas, a sports reporter for 15min.lt.

In Lithuania, nothing was too familiar to the Ball brothers, but their new patriarch resembled somebody they knew well. Seskus served as the unofficial general manager of the Balls' new team, Prienai Vytautas, and was free to run the club as he saw fit. He had already lifted his club from the Lithuanian minor league to the major domestic league called the LKL. "He's like a God out there," quipped one prominent European agent.

Seskus also brandishes an unpredictable temper, according to former players. He shuts down practices early and sometimes forces his teams to play soccer instead of shooting hoops. Another tactic he employed was to pull his players off the court in the middle of the game, a move LaVar himself had used in an AAU game during the summer. Recent gold medalist for Jeff Van Gundy and Team USA at the 2017 FIBA AmeriCup, former Canisius guard, Billy Baron fondly remembered: "We'd come out to the parking lot after practices and Coach (Seskus) was there selling meat to players out of the trunk of his car. Some players actually bought that stuff from him."

"Virginijus Seskus is crazy," said one of his former players, Mike Moser, who was a one-time All-American honorable mention with the Runnin' Rebels of UNLV and spent a single season in Vilnius playing under Seskus. "I'm trying to erase that year from my memory. I've been around the world—Lithuania, Israel, Kosovo, Italy, and Qatar—I had good coaches; he wasn't one of them. I don't care if you're a rookie or a vet, he's hard to play for. He used to get so mad and kick balls in practice. He was always yelling and cursing for no reason, even at the locals. If he coaches the same, those boys, LiAngelo and LaMelo, will be home within a month," Moser concluded.

He wasn't far off the mark as LaVar pulled the plug on the Baltic experience after three months. "We're not going to waste our time no more," reasoned the typically forthright Ball senior, pointing to an injury to LiAngelo and scant playing time for LaMelo. How did Seskus rate LaMelo during his stopover in Lithuania? While "Melo is still young" and had some "good experience because he was so bold", the playmaking guard "also has to understand that you have to play defense a bit," the coach determined. Melo finished his LKL season with averages of 6.5 points and 2.4 assists, shooting 26.8 percent from the field in 12.8 minutes per game.

What did Melo manage to gain from his limited on-court time there? "I feel it helped me in the long run. I grew up a lot. After doing that, I felt I could go anywhere," Melo insisted. Lithuania was mostly a crash course for the Ball brothers in the lifestyle of making it as a pro ballplayer. Take a glance at the family's Facebook show, "Ball in the Family," to witness how the Balls lived in Lithuania. It was a fiasco, but it served as a learning experience that Melo could rely on when he made his way to the National Basketball League (NBL) in Australia—as far off as Lithuania, but perhaps not so frigid.

LaMelo didn't slide out of Lithuania so easily either. On "*Outside The Lines,"* ESPN's Jeff Goodman communicated conversations he had with the Ball brothers' former Vytautas teammates. LaMelo came off as "lazy" and "arrogant". Goodman concluded, "For LaMelo, it wasn't very good. He barely played in the Lithuanian League games. One former teammate described him to me earlier today as 'lazy' and 'arrogant.' Wasn't really engaged in the whole process. (He) played undisciplined, which we've seen in AAU ball. But (he) didn't really get better. And that's the goal over there: for a 16-year-old to improve and get better. Multiple people I talked to on that team, on Vytautas, said LaMelo really never bought in."

Never mind that LaMelo was just 16 at the time, trying to play in a league that's far from Europe's best, but does showcase plenty of talented players who are more experienced and much bigger than the lanky LaMelo. At the end of the day, Melo made just eight appearances for the 8-24 Vytautas squad (according to RealGM.com) and was clearly ready to go home— or at least move on to his dad's following favorite locale. After all was said and done, LaMelo was declared "the youngest American professional basketball player ever". He was the first 16-year-old with a signature shoe, the Melo Ball 1, and counts

Golden State MVPs, Stephen Curry and Kevin Durant among his myriad social media followers.

Sports reporter, Urbonas, clarified how the Balls' time in Lithuania could be divided into three distinct periods. After the initial euphoria, it became increasingly clear that LaMelo was not cut out for the level of competition on offer—or at least not yet. "The second part was kind of coming back to reality. Watching it, we started following more closely. We wanted to see how LaMelo was performing on the court—if LiAngelo was good, and he actually was pretty good. He was very, very underrated coming into Lithuania. We probably thought that LaMelo might contribute more because we saw more potential in Melo's game. Gelo is three years older and he's more mature for the pro game, but still, we expected more from Melo," Urbonas related.

But when boredom started to set in as a result of the Ball brothers' lack of success (and perhaps the difficulty the coaches and media had handling the "boisterous" elder Ball), the numbers in terms of actual game attendance and on social media took a serious tumble. Urbanos continued, "The third month was kind of sad. I don't know if you noticed, but during the games that we broadcast on Facebook, you could tell that there weren't many people in the stands. Also, the Facebook numbers decreased a lot. Compared to the first games where we had more than 100,000 people watching, in the end, it was like five or 6,000 people. It was a picture of the overall attention in Lithuania. We got bored; people got bored mostly because we saw that LaMelo can't perform at the pro level yet and most of the people were irritated with the LaVar and Coach Seskus stuff that hurt the team. Also, some of the players had a bad approach to LaMelo and LiAngelo, so these inside conflicts were damaging to the overall image in Lithuania."

One particular game stood out, but not due to any high-flying dunks by the Ball brothers. When Vytautas squared off against the best Lithuanian team, Zalgiris, which had previously played in the EuroLeague Final Four (Europe's most prestigious tournament), LaVar was desperate for both brothers to start against the best opponents. At the same time, Coach Seskus didn't deem the two among the five best or toughest that he needed on the court to win the game. "The thing is, they actually played a really good game against Zalgiris. They just didn't start, which in Europe isn't really a big business. Sometimes good players are not starting, and who cares because they are playing the crucial minutes and being a game-changing factor," Urbonas explained.

If you hadn't already guessed, LaVar was livid and didn't want to listen to anybody, according to Urbonas. The Lithuanian reporter mentioned the possibility of the language barrier, or possibly a cultural barrier, saying that "European basketball is unique in its own way." Seskus just couldn't find a way to explain his decisions to LaVar, as numerous other coaches haven't and won't, and the plug was effectively pulled. (1,561)

[Part 5: Los Angeles Ballers]

Most of us are happy to spend four years at the same high school and maybe even four more at the same college or university. But most don't have a dad quite like LaVar. Not long after LaMelo's Lithuania gig, his father announced the formation of the Junior Basketball Association (JBA) in the summer of 2018, made to order for his two youngest sons. The blueprint of the league was "to serve as a bridge between high school and the NBA as an alternative route to NCAA basketball". For the one season the JBA managed to survive, its eight teams offered a few chosen kids the early opportunity to play pro ball stateside.

Some of the youngsters that LaVar's fledgling league promised to help included smooth-shooting Gregory Floyd, who lost his NCAA Division 1 scholarship when his school grades tanked after the sudden death of his sister, Nate Morris, who was booted off the U. of Mississippi team after DUI and speeding tickets with a high-flyer, Nyang Wek, from South Sudan, who was kicked out of his Mississippi high school squad "for dating a girl who was a different race" than him. Common consensus has it that Hoops allows many athletes to get a college education, but the truly limited number of options many have is not often discussed. However, before long, the league ran into a range of problems, from missed payments to low attendance to not enough talent. Then, when LaMelo found yet another alternative route to the NCAA, which took the form of the NBL, the JBA's days were numbered. Ball's league turned out to a blip on the NCAA and NBA radars, which disappeared as quickly as it had burst on the scene.

For a brief period, the JBA did provide some players with another legitimate outlet to play games, practice, and focus on basketball rather than schooling. Yet the Next Stars program associated with the NBL in Australia became a stronger alternative, but not before LiAngelo and LaMelo had some fun balling in the JBA. Melo was 17 at the time, one of the youngest in the league, and rated as a top open-court player, with deep but low-percentage range, dreadful defensive habits, as well as lacking the vision and explosiveness shown by the older brother, Lonzo, at the same age.

The JBA had its day, created by LaVar's constant hype and further gassed by their reality show on Facebook, as all league games were broadcast on its FB channel. Most of the games recorded between 100,000 and 200,000 views, whereas Melo's outings with the LA Ballers had closer to 800K. Those impressive stats contrasted sharply with the actual fan count with tickets starting at $39 (by the way, the Big Baller sneakers cost a pretty penny at $495 a pair at that juncture). A typical game might draw 300 fans to the stands, including 100 fans settling into the courtside seats that cost $99 per person.

JBA co-owner, Alan Foster, didn't care too much about the fan count. "What's happening on this court is cute and all. But that content up there?" said Foster, pointing to the video feed on the giant scoreboard. "That stuff on your phone? That's what we're talking about. The experience for the viewers is what it's about," he stated while claiming more than a million views per game, and then listing a lucrative group of tentative Fortune 500 advertisers.

Labeled from the start as the JBA's "marquee player," LaMelo had little choice but to light it up. On May 4, 2018, he inked a contract with the LA Ballers, and on June 21, racked up a triple-double in his league debut: 40 points, 16 boards, 10 assists, plus three steals, shooting 15-of-40 from the field. LA snagged a 134-124 win over the Ballers from New York. In the regular season, which consisted of eight games, Melo averaged a triple-double with 39.6 points, 14.6 rebounds, and 11.5 assists per game and was naturally selected to the All-Star Game. The aforementioned Floyd, 19, got out on the break with Melo in LA. He spent his first JBA paycheck ($1,178 after taxes) for mostly "clothes and snacks" while hoping to catch on with the NBA or maybe overseas, and then "I guess get into coaching".

Moving on to the playoff semis again versus the NY. Melo soared even higher with a season-high 55 points, 16 boards, and seven assists. Finally, he helped bring the championship home to LA with a Finals victory against the Seattle Ballers, though

LiAngelo was the man with 58 points in that game, while Melo chipped in nine assists. After the game, LaVar posed for a lot of pretty pictures, signed stuff for a long line of excited fans, and granted an exclusive interview, while the reality show cameras caught it all. ESPN's TheUndefeated reporter, Jesse Washington, challenged Ball, claiming that his league could turn kids off from getting an education—young hoopsters who had little or no chance of making real cash as pros. LaVar countered, "If you've been playing basketball all your life, you want to get on that platform. You think you're a pro? Come to this league. Now if you don't have no more eligibility and all that, that's fine too. You still can go back to school."

Washington spoke up again, "But you'd have to pay for an education you could have gotten for free." LaVar was quick with his comeback: "OK. Go work for it. Go work for it. You couldn't have gotten it for free because you were coming to play basketball anyway. You bring these guys in and you bring them for athletics. Let's say he is averaging one point and one rebound, but he's a 4.0 student. You got to go. But if you average 25 and 22, guess what? We'll get you a tutor."

Ball was trying to show that the players don't ever get a "free" education as they truly trade their labor for it, the kind of labor that creates billions of dollars of revenue for the large schools, while in return, the players only gain the cost of tuition, room and board, and some expenses. With the JBA, Ball was indeed hyping the hypocrisy of big-time university sports.

He went on to point out that all eight players on the JBA championship (which happened to include two of his sons) would be gifted a new car. He continued by promising to take the league's 10 best on a European tour to highlight their talent. He vowed to pay top recruits $10,000, $20,000, $50,000 a month, plus 60 percent of their shirt sales. The elder Ball pledged that all the best hoopsters would opt for the JBA rather than college or the G League: "Because I'm the Big Baller and they don't know who the boss is in the G League. Because my league is real. These dudes are going to come through this lane. They are going to be like, 'Man, he is so genuine. That is who I want to play for.'"

On the flip side, Ball was also quick to say that if a player wasn't pro-ready, he'd be sent home in a snap. And he avoided saying that those players sent home wouldn't have any college eligibility left. It was all quite real for a select few as the so-called "JBA USA" squad jetted off to Europe to face a few teams. Then, on October 31, in a "friendly" game versus Dzukija (in Lithuania of all places), Melo was ejected when he slapped an opponent in the face during an altercation. Five days later, the youngest Baller left the JBA tour to get back to SPIRE for his impending senior season. LaMelo capped it by saying, "I thank my dad for the JBA experience and playing overseas."

MELO'S RECRUITMENT

Granted, the LaMelo Ball story skips around a bit, so thanks for sticking with it. At the tender age of 13, LaMelo committed "verbally" to play college hoops for UCLA, the third in a line of Ball brothers to do so. Although he was also being courted by Virginia and Washington State at the time, Melo made it publicly clear that UCLA was his "dream school". In his sophomore year of high school, he was labeled a top "five-star" recruit in the 2019 graduating class, as well as a premier point guard. Even after a professional stint in 2018, he remained on the five-star recruiting list.

Lonzo played college hoops for the Bruins for a single season, earning consensus first-team All-American honors before bolting for the Lakers. LiAngelo was a freshman on the Bruins team when he was cuffed for shoplifting on tour in China, together with teammates, Cody Riley and Jalen Hill, before any of them could play a single game for the university. When news of his indefinite suspension from UCLA hit the airwaves, LaVar quickly decided to yank his second son from the prestigious halls of Westwood, saying that he hadn't been treated so badly even in China.

"You shouldn't hang them on the cross for this long for that," Ball lamented on CNN. "A kid wants to play basketball all his life. You take that away, that's worse than jail. Why should we as parents and adults keep jumping on them? It's not like we're going through life without making mistakes... China already forgave the boys. They returned it. Why keep them from playing sports and take their meal passes? You already sent a message. They already apologized. What's the big deal?"

Notwithstanding, LaVar vowed to transform LiAngelo into an NBAer quickly enough. "I'm going to make him way better for the draft than UCLA could ever have. He's not transferring to another school. The plan is now to get Gelo ready for the NBA draft," Mr. Ball concluded. The fact that LaVar had already pulled Melo from Chino Hills High School and then had him play against pro competition in Lithuania and the JBA made his chances of playing as a Bruin ever slimmer. However, he apparently hadn't been compensated while in the aforementioned leagues, and his return to SPIRE for his senior year as a prep student gave a glimmer of hope to UCLA boosters.

The release of the Melo Ball 1 signature sneaker in 2017 by the family's sports apparel company, Big Baller Brand, seemed to seal the deal. The National Collegiate Athletic Association or NCAA didn't look lightly on LaVar's willful dismissal of eligibility rules. Furthermore, the fact that Melo soon signed with an agent (Harrison Gaines, 28 years old at the time, who also represented Lonzo) set him back even further, forcing him to look at alternative options, including the NBA G League and pro leagues in Australia and China.

The Big Baller brand shoe was the clearest violation of NCAA rules on amateurism. "The NCAA's not going to clear (LaMelo) because he's got a shoe right now, a sneaker where he's making money off of," ESPN's Jeff Goodman stressed on "Outside the Lines". The legal question of who was really making money off the shoe (Melo himself or the family brand) remained open to discussion. But after LaMelo announced he'd be back for his senior year at SPIRE and claimed he would like to play at least a year of college ball and was "targeting" the likes of Duke, North Carolina, Kansas, Kentucky, and Michigan State, he had attorneys, lawyers, and NCAA experts scrambling.

"I've never seen a confluence of so many issues in one case, but I still do think it's workable," attorney, Don Jackson, chimed in. "Every one of these issues standing alone—agents, money from a shoe company, playing with a pro team, endorsements—is not an amateur career-ending infraction. When you have all of those issues colliding in one case, that makes it more complicated, but I don't think it makes it impossible."

Even though Melo clearly touted his signature shoe in showy photos and videos, if he were proven to have accepted no money directly, he might somehow be off the hook with the NCAA. Even the presence of an agent is now sometimes excusable for an amateur player if he were deemed to possess "elite" status under new USA Basketball guidelines (although the fact that agent Gaines brokered the deal directly with

Lithuanian club, Vytautas, on Twitter before the NCAA rule change could also quash that).

In the end, it didn't matter. Melo played a season at SPIRE, headed off to Lithuania to play briefly as a pro, made it back to LA to be a JBA Baller for a season, and then set off as far and wide as he could to the land "Down Under" where he could gain seasoning in one of the best non-NBA leagues in the world. China was the only other choice that would have offered Melo substantial minutes (and the chance to pad his stats against lesser competition). LaVar made his boy's move to Oz sound relatively simple when he said, "You've got to go to Lithuania—where sights are not as good, it's cold, guys are talking bad about you, you don't understand the language—to enjoy all this. You can see the happiness on my son's face right now, and it's beautiful. Melo just wants to play basketball. He'd play basketball on the moon."

ILLAWARRA HAWKS

On June 17, 2019, Ball signed a two-year deal, including "NBA out clauses," with the Illawarra Hawks of the Australian-based National Basketball League (NBL) located in Wollogong, not far south of Sydney. He was able to join the Hawks through the NBL "Next Stars" program, which aims to nurture NBA draft prospects. In August 2019, after playing for the No Shnacks in the Drew League (a Pro-Am summer league in LA), Ball was named "Leader of the New School," an award that recognizes the league's best rookie. In advance of the NBL season, he headed to Australia with his former SPIRE Institute coach, Jermaine Jackson, who became his agent and manager and assisted Melo with the adaptation process.

Ball used the 12 games he played in Australia's premier league to boost his NBA draft stock. He had fallen out of clear sight without NCAA eligibility and US exposure. But NBA scouts who made the voyage to see Ball in action considered the upside he showed against 20- and 30-year-old vets as sufficient for a nod as the No. 1 pick in June's NBA draft. Then Coronavirus came along and threw a wrench and more into everybody's plans. Miraculously, a truncated NBA season was played inside an Orlando "bubble" in October and the draft was pushed back to November.

Kyle Kuzma (who turned out to be a champion with the LA Lakers in that very bubble was also a former teammate of Lonzo's, and continues to be a pal to the Ball brothers) was also in Australia for the FIBA World Cup in September. Without a hint of sarcasm, he had this to say just before LaMelo's sojourn Down Under: "I think this is the right move for him. He's a special talent, a guy that a lot of people are really watching. I think that he has a lot of potentials to do a lot of great things. Being here in Australia is probably going to be one of the best things for him, playing in the NBL, which is one of the top leagues in the world. I think the fans in Australia are going to be happy to see him and the crowds are probably going to be crazy. I think it's just good for the league and good for the global game."

The Hawks themselves were set to enjoy a new phase with the head coach, Matt Flinn, joining Ball as rookie members of the franchise. Showcasing a premier player like Melo and allowing a dynamic coach like Flinn to take over quickly created lots of excitement and a fresh culture for a team without a title since the turn of the decade. LaMelo was only in Australia for a week but had already established certain alchemy with his Hawks. The first time Melo spoke publicly since landing halfway around the world, he appeared briefly for the media in an Illawarra jersey. With as much enthusiasm as he's capable off the court, he claimed, "They're real nice guys. I feel we've got good chemistry with them already. Everybody wants to talk, everybody wants to hang out, so it's all a great bond. Everybody trains hard. It seems like a winning culture here, so that's what we want to do."

The hooping wasn't bad at first. In late September, he had success at the NBL Blitz, a pre-season tournament. He recorded 19 points, 13 boards, and 7 assists in a preseason win over the Perth Wildcats. On October 6, in his first regular-season game, Ball notched 12 points, 10 rebounds, and five assists on 6-of-17 shooting in a loss to the Brisbane Bullets. He really had to get in gear after a season-ending injury to star point guard, Aaron Brooks, on October 27. So Ball blazed for a season-high 32 points, 11 rebounds, and 13 assists on November 25 in an OT victory over the Cairns Taipans, the youngest NBL player to record a triple-double.

Ball followed his first with another triple-double (25 points, 12 rebounds, and 10 assists), but was limited to 10-of-28 shooting in a tough loss to the New Zealand Breakers. He became only the fourth player in the history of the NBL, and the first since the league changed to 40-minute games in 2009, to grab consecutive triple-doubles.

But on December 8, before he played another game, news came that Melo would miss four weeks of Aussie hoops after bruising his foot during practice. Then on January 16, 2020, still sidelined, the youngest Ball announced he would sit out the rest of the season. He split with the Hawks on January 28 to return to the US, apparently to prep for the 2020 NBA Draft. In his 12 NBL games, Melo averaged 17 points,

7.4 rebounds, and 6.8 assists per game, while shooting 37.7 percent from the field. From beyond the three-point strip, Melo was an anemic 25%, but he was heralded for his play-making, court vision, and the triple-double threat he posed. At the end of the season, he was awarded the NBL Rookie of the Year trophy, nipping Sudanese-Australian Kouat Noi by five votes (49 to 44).

The league's regular season wrapped up at the end of February and the Hawks (5-17) were far from post-season contention. Thus, there was no need to rush back for only a two- or three-week spell. "Melo's foot is totally healed, but the doctor's policy is if you're out for six weeks, you must rehab for six weeks," Jackson related to ESPN. "He's starting court work tomorrow."

You might not have guessed that Melo wasn't finished with the Hawks. Contrary to the way he wore out his welcome in Lithuania, ESPN soon reported that Melo and Jermaine Jackson had decided to buy the Illawarra franchise soon after his departure. Financial woes had troubled the Hawks, but apparently no more. The exact purchase price wasn't immediately known, but other teams like the Brisbane Bullets had been up for sale recently for between $5 and $10 million, according to Financial Review, and Melbourne United had been allegedly sold for $10 million. In fact, the entire league had been sold to a gentleman named Larry Kestelman in 2015 for the grand total of $7 million (which compares quite favorably to the sale of a single NBA franchise called the LA Clippers who were purchased for $2 billion in August, 2014, part of former Microsoft hotshot, Steve Ballmer's $28.5 billion net worth).

While still only 18 years of age, Melo had already enjoyed several revenue streams for a few years. His NBL contract wasn't made public, but ESPN previously claimed that players were paid at least $78K in the Next Stars program. The family reality show on Facebook, "Ball In The Family," had already appeared for five seasons with more than 100 episodes shown, and Melo's more than 5.6 million Instagram followers were definitely worth something to someone. The main wonder at the moment is how much Melo can haul in as a top-five pick in the NBA Draft.

Zion Williamson cashed in on a guaranteed $44 million as the top 2019 pick (assuming of course that his two optional years on the deal's back end are picked up). The number five pick from a year ago, Darius Garland, was guaranteed a cool $29 million over four years. Melo can expect as much, but he'll really roll in the dough from endorsements. These deals should help the young man feed the racehorse he recently bought and named LaMelo.

To tell the truth, Ball wasn't the only former top high school recruit who headed to the NBL instead of playing college hoops. Another five-star prospect, R.J. Hampton, signed with the New Zealand Breakers and should be a lottery pick in the 2020 draft. "When high school kids hear LaMelo owns the team, they will want to come," Jackson affirmed. "They'll know they'll be taken care of. We're going to put the organization on steroids, building it into a program that guys want to play for. I'm in touch with several former GMs who want to go there to help out, including high-level coaches who won every championship you can imagine." Jackson himself had spent several stints with NBA teams like the Bucks and Knicks, as well as the illustrious CBA's Great Lakes Storm.

Melo's limited presence in the NBL helped the league to set viewership and attendance records. League head, Kestelman, stated that the NBL managed to haul in $1.4 billion in global media contracts after the Melo man came to town.

MELO PUMA DEAL

LaVar tried to keep a stiff upper lip when Melo announced he was leaving his father's (and family's) Big Baller Brand to sign a lucrative deal with rival Puma in August, 2020. Perhaps "rival" isn't the best choice of words as BBB never challenged Adidas, Nike, or Puma in any serious way for sports shoe supremacy. At first, LaVar seemed supportive of Melo's departure and even said that the door was open for his son to return to BBB in the future. But reality shows tend to show what's real, and sure enough, "Ball in The Family" caught LaVar's true anger and frustration as his second son wanted his freedom (Lonzo also announced he was on the lookout for another sneaker deal, far from BBB).

Producer: "Do you agree with Melo's decision?"

LaVar: "Oh no. Definitely not, because, look, I've been priming my boys from day one. 'Don't sign no endorsement deal. Don't do that because they going to own you.' Everybody's stuck on this. They want me to be mad because LaMelo signed with Puma. I don't want the narrative to be: I'm against my boy. And he's 19 now, so he's going to do [expletive] his own way. Just like the [expletive] told me '[expletive] you, I'm going to do it my own way.' He doesn't see the freedom that he has. It's a [expletive] Puma shoe. That [expletive] don't say LaMelo Ball on it."

It's a fact that LaMelo's Puma deal doesn't give him the "ownership" that LaVar mentions and the control he would continue to have by sticking with the family brand, but the young Ball apparently will rake in more than $100 million and be able to fly around in the company jet when he pleases as well. In addition, it's still possible for Melo to have his own signature clothes and shoe line inside the big Puma brand in the future.

"I'm (a) one of one," LaMelo Ball exclaims. "I do whatever I want." Ball talks with the kind of confidence you'd expect from a 19-year-old prodigy who is light years ahead in his field. Still, even though this top NBA prospect exudes confidence, it's tainted by the rawness of a first-year university student, wide-eyed about what he or she could encounter in a career and life. Not too many of us at that age already owned a pro sports team we once played for or had celebrity parents who included us in a reality TV show about family "secrets" seen by millions, or were asked to endorse a huge global brand before playing in a solitary NBA game.

Puma's Global Director of Brand and Marketing, Adam Petrick, didn't confirm the cash involved in the contract, but he was available to provide some details about the plane. "Puma does have a jet that we use for many of our players and, of course, he'll have access to that jet," Petrick clarified, adding that the financial details of all endorsements are strictly confidential. "The value of our contracts sometimes comes down to agents inflating dollars, and that's okay. It is what it is, and it's part of the culture."

Petrick was also in charge of the brand's partnerships with Rihanna, Jay Z, and a few other slightly-less-famous individuals. He admitted that Puma's interest in LaMelo was pushed by the player's youthful energy and rebellious attitude. "Melo doesn't want to be seen in the same light as everyone else and he gravitates toward the idea of not being normal," Petrick affirmed. "He doesn't want to be every other player that's out there, and I think that Puma reflects that."

Melo made it clear that running and dunking with Puma was a better platform for him, although he had a range of sneaker brands to select from. The oldest brother, Lonzo, was the first "face" of the family's BBB, but he then negotiated a 2019 deal with Nike. "My brother gives me advice every day and he told me to pretty much take it all in," LaMelo said about Lonzo who wasn't allowed to have meetings with any other sneaker brand before making it in the NBA. "With everything Puma is doing in the culture, it just fits me and what I was trying to do."

Puma has basketball roots going way back to the 1970s (which was the last time the NY Knicks, with Senator Bill Bradley, Clyde "The Glide" Frazier, Earl "The Pearl" Monroe, and Phil Jackson, last won a championship, if you didn't know), but only really re-entered the category two years ago. For its hoops rebirth, Puma has primarily concentrated on signing younger, rising players like the Lakers' Kyle Kuzma, and the Denver Nuggets' Michael Porter, Jr. They also grabbed some vets like LA's Danny Green, San Antonio's Rudy Gay, and WNBA star, Skylar Diggins-Smith to sport their shoes.

In addition, the multinational brand has been making moves in the culture surrounding the game, like hiring Jay Z to be Puma Basketball's creative director and hiring rap singer, J. Cole to endorse the label. "We're trying to be more than typical on-court performance," Petrick claims. "Performance is obviously the basis of everything, but for us, it's about culture. It's about style. It's about what happens beyond the court that makes Puma different. And I think that seems to match Melo. We can do whatever we want to shake things up and really have a challenger mentality."

Melo himself muses on Twitter, "I personally chose a different path to achieve my success because that defines who I am. I know some people think I'm mysterious or 'not from here', and I might have to agree. I am someone who likes to be different and consider myself to be 1 of 1." Petrick then said he could surely see signature LaMelo stuff like clothes and shoes coming down the line. The plan is to promote the player both on and off the basketball court. "It's gotta be something that's me and helps me express who I am," Ball declared while imagining what a possible LaMelo x Puma collection could look like. Then again, nobody ever imagined a 19-year-old Melo quite like this.

NOVEMBER 19, 2020: NEW YORK CITY, USA

A few years after LaVar Ball bragged that he could bust the world-famous GOAT (the "Greatest Of All Time" that many now consider Jordan following his six NBA championships with the Chicago Bulls) playing one-on-one, the Charlotte Hornets and their majority owner, Michael Jordan decided to draft 19-year-old LaMelo Ball (and his family and entourage) as the Number 3 pick in the 2020 NBA Draft—after much hand-wringing. Jordan has been criticized for some of his dud draft picks in previous years, but LaMelo Ball looks to be "the real deal".

According to Sports Illustrated, Ball was the right choice for the Hornets and the organization will focus on developing him into "an All-Star-level centerpiece". Ball has great size for his position (point guard), but more critically, he's a visionary playmaker who thrives on the open floor. He's the kind of expressive talent that Charlotte's roster has really been missing. If Melo can work to improve his jump shot, he will be extremely difficult to stop. And if the Hornets can find the right players to put around him, Ball can be "the straw that stirs the drink" (as they used to say about the Yankees' slugger, Reggie Jackson) or the engine that drives their rebuilding efforts.

Although the Hornets run a risk here, Ball represents fantastic value at the No. 3 pick, and is a player the Hornets and their fans should be excited about. One thing is for sure: no matter what he does as a rookie, the spotlight will always be on him.

MORE FROM JACKSON CARTER BIOGRAPHIES

My goal is to spark the love of reading in young adults around the world. Too often children grow up thinking they hate reading because they are forced to read material they don't care about. To counter this we offer accessible, easy to read biographies about sportspeople that will give young adults the chance to fall in love with reading.

Go to the Website Below to Join Our Community

https://mailchi.mp/7cced1339ff6/jcbcommunity

Or Find Us on Facebook at

www.facebook.com/JacksonCarterBiographies

As a Member of Our Community You Will Receive:

First Notice of Newly Published Titles

Exclusive Discounts and Offers

Influence on the Next Book Topics

Don't miss out, join today and help spread the love of reading around the world!

OTHER WORKS BY JACKSON CARTER BIOGRAPHIES

Patrick Mahomes: The Amazing Story of How Patrick Mahomes Became the MVP of the NFL

Donovan Mitchell: How Donovan Mitchell Became a Star for the Salt Lake City Jazz

Luka Doncic: The Complete Story of How Luka Doncic Became the NBA's Newest Star

The Eagle: Khabib Nurmagomedov: How Khabib Became the Top MMA Fighter and Dominated the UFC

Lamar Jackson: The Inspirational Story of How One Quarterback Redefined the Position and Became the Most Explosive Player in the NFL

Jimmy Garoppolo: The Amazing Story of How One Quarterback Climbed the Ranks to Be One of the Top Quarterbacks in the NFL

Zion Williamson: The Inspirational Story of How Zion Williamson Became the NBA's First Draft Pick

Kyler Murray: The Inspirational Story of How Kyler Murray Became the NFL's First Draft Pick

Do Your Job: The Leadership Principles that Bill Belichick and the New England Patriots Have Used to Become the Best Dynasty in the NFL

Turn Your Gaming Into a Career Through Twitch and Other Streaming Sites: How to Start, Develop and Sustain an Online Streaming Business that Makes Money

From Beginner to Pro: How to Become a Notary Public

Printed in Great Britain
by Amazon

14063513R00031